B2

E4-95

Sunset of British Steam

Sunset of British Steam

John Vaughan

OXFORD PUBLISHING COMPANY

© Oxford Publishing Co. and John Vaughan
SBN 86093 163 3

Frontispiece

Plate 1   Although this volume illustrates those four sad years at the end of steam on BR, this photograph shows that not all the locomotives featured have been scrapped. Some, like 'Merchant Navy' Class Pacific No. 35028 *Clan Line*, have been preserved and restored to main line running. On 2nd March 1966 the impressive modified machine thunders through Weybridge with a down express to Bournemouth.

Title page

Plate 2   The Isle of Wight railways provided the old-world charm of the Victorian era. The appropriately named Class O2 0-4-4T No. 16 *Ventnor* enters Ventnor station, as the driver of a train from Ryde passes the token to the signalman on the exit from Ventnor tunnel, under St. Boniface Down.

All photographs reproduced in this volume were taken by the author.

Printed by Bocardo & Church Army Press Ltd. in the City of Oxford

Bound by Kemp Hall Bindery, Oxford

Published by:
Oxford Publishing Co.,
8 The Roundway,
Headington, Oxford

INTRODUCTION

It is hard to believe that sixteen years have now elapsed since the last steam locomotive was seen in service on some regions of British Rail, and over thirteen years have passed since the last fire was dropped from a steam locomotive running in normal service on BR standard gauge lines. For those who lived through those last years and experienced the gradual rundown of steam power, the period will be extremely nostalgic and filled with sadness. It is easy to remember the past glories of steam, with gleaming locomotives painted in the liveries of the private railway companies, and even the post-nationalisation period, when at least most express passenger engines carried nameplates, and all locomotives had number plates. But although those final years will be remembered, it is easy to forget just how bad the condition of the dwindling ranks of survivors was, as they hung on by a thread in a filthy matt black livery, with steam leaking from every joint and with all removable proof of identity either removed or stolen. It is this final period, from the autumn of 1964 until the late summer of 1968, which is the subject of this volume, the final chapter in the story of British steam in everyday service.

In trying to convey the general atmosphere of those final years of steam, I have divided this book into a number of mini subject headings. They show the railway scene from various viewpoints, and concentrate on the less common photographic locations. Although main lines, branch lines, engine sheds and general subjects are included, the usual locations of Shap and Sonning will not be found. In any event, by late 1964, the choice of locations was restricted, and complete counties were totally devoid of steam. The number of classes of locomotive in service had contracted by the mid 1960s and, with some notable exceptions, most pre-grouping examples had become extinct. For the steam enthusiast this did not detract from the attraction of the railways, because any steam sighting was an event in those final days, and scores of hours could be spent lineside without a single opportunity of recording the iron horse on film.

All regions are represented in this volume, but with steam finishing on the Western Region as early as 31st December 1965, closely followed by the Scottish and Eastern Regions, there is, inevitably, some emphasis on the Southern and London Midland Regions. The majority of the 250 photographs, reproduced herein, have not been published before and over forty classes of locomotive are featured. Whilst the steam scene lent itself to creative and progressive photography, I have tried to balance the traditional with the artistic in conveying the decadent atmosphere of the period. Steam sheds were always moody places and many depots are featured. The men of steam, the railwaymen themselves, are not forgotten, and 'men at work' are featured. I have deliberately avoided using photographs of steam locomotives being cut up, although some illustrations of dead machinery, in the final hours, have been included. It is a tribute to the simple, but rugged, design of the steam locomotive, that many of the machines continued to run until the end with almost non-existent maintenance, and a degree of mistreatment. Happily the preservationists have ensured that future generations will continue to enjoy the sight and sound of the steam engine in the United Kingdom, but the period of rundown and dilapidation covered by this volume will never be repeated.

On a personal note, I must draw attention to the sociological change of the past decade or two, whereby enthusiasts now often travel the length of the country in a single day to attend an event, or observe a railway happening. Many of these photographs were taken in conditions of comparative hardship. I distinctly recall travelling from the Sussex coast to the North East on a small single cylinder 'James' motorcycle in order to photograph Class J27s working in County Durham, and facing the elements during the two day journey. I can also remember saving for some weeks in order to visit the Manchester area for a few days. Most firms allowed their employees only two weeks holiday a year, and the casual day off was frowned upon. A detailed knowledge of railway workings was limited, and non existent in some areas, and there were no TOPS computer terminals available with access to information, so saving what could well have been an abortive journey. Except for workings over famous inclines, it was impossible to guarantee that locomotives would be working on a particular piece of urban freight line selected for a day's photography. There would be no pre-arranged overfills on water troughs, no carefully provided black smoke, as some groups of young photographers might have expected. These photographs are unrehearsed impressions of the steam scene, taken on photographic equipment which was good but simple, compared with today's sophisticated kit. I was one of the earlier exponents of the telephoto lens in railway photography, in order to increase pictorial impression or improve composition. It is strange to relate that during the sometimes frantic search for working steam, the early classes of diesel locomotive were completely ignored, and yet, many of them have now passed into railway history. Such is the path of progress, I sincerely hope that those who experienced the end of BR steam will enjoy this volume, and that it will provoke many recollections. I would like to think that these photographs convey to those who missed those final years, an accurate portrayal without embellishment or glorification.

I particularly wish to thank OPC for the freedom extended to me, in selecting and arranging the photographic content of this volume. The book is dedicated to all my close railway photographer colleagues, whose friendship has been much appreciated over the years, but especially to the 'Morrison Gap' — the period covered by this volume, when one of the leading railway photographers of our time temporarily hung up his camera and allowed some of the youngsters to become established. Finally, my wife Carol deserves special mention for understanding why, by coincidence, our marriage took place shortly *after* the end of steam on BR!

John A. M. Vaughan
Dorking
November 1981

TRAFFORD PARK

Plate 3 Trafford Park shed, or 9E according to the smokebox doors, was situated on the old Cheshire Lines Committee route out of Manchester. It was a busy shed, but activity was at a minimum on 12th September 1967 when this photograph was taken. A serviceable Class 8F 2-8-0 No. 48269 stands beside unserviceable No. 42656, one of the last Stanier 2-6-4Ts to remain in service.

Plate 4 With some antique signals in the background, 'Black Five' No. 45316 pounds past the Trafford Park sidings with a heavy freight from the Liverpool direction. Most freight trains in this era were either loose coupled or vacuum braked.

Plate 5 Framed by a water column in the land of ▶ London Midland tapered boilers, is a grimy No. 44708. Nearly 850 of these mixed traffic locomotives saw service on every region of BR during their 34 year life span, although many of the class were built after the war.

Plate 6 With top feed pipes removed and standing alone on the grease encrusted rails, is No. 45420. This locomotive had worked in the Manchester area for several years, but was not always allocated to Trafford Park.

Plate 7 Maunsell-designed SE&CR N Class locomotives lasted into 1966, and bearing in mind that original examples were introduced as long ago as 1917, this was quite an achievement. Leaving Eastleigh, tender first, with coach set number 839 is No. 31842 in April 1965.

Plate 8   The last of the Southern pre-nationalisation Mogul 2-6-0s ended up at Guildford motive power depot. In this photograph, Class 5 No. 73082 *Camelot*, one of the Standards to receive names from withdrawn 'King Arthur' Class locomotives, is hauling the last U Class 2-6-0 No. 31639, N Class No. 31408 and Standard 4-6-0 No. 73170 past Worplesdon to their final resting place, on 1st July 1966.

Plate 9   With the foreground dominated by nine old-pattern luggage barrows, one of the last working N Class locomotives, No. 31411, shunts the yard at Fareham, Hampshire, in August 1965. The bay platform here, was once used by trains on the now abandoned Meon Valley line to Alton.

Plate 10   Another 1965 scene at Eastleigh, with No. 31873 enjoying some bright winter sunshine as it takes its share of coal and water. These mixed traffic locomotives turned the scales at 61 tons, had a 200 lb boiler pressure and 5 ft 6 ins driving wheels.

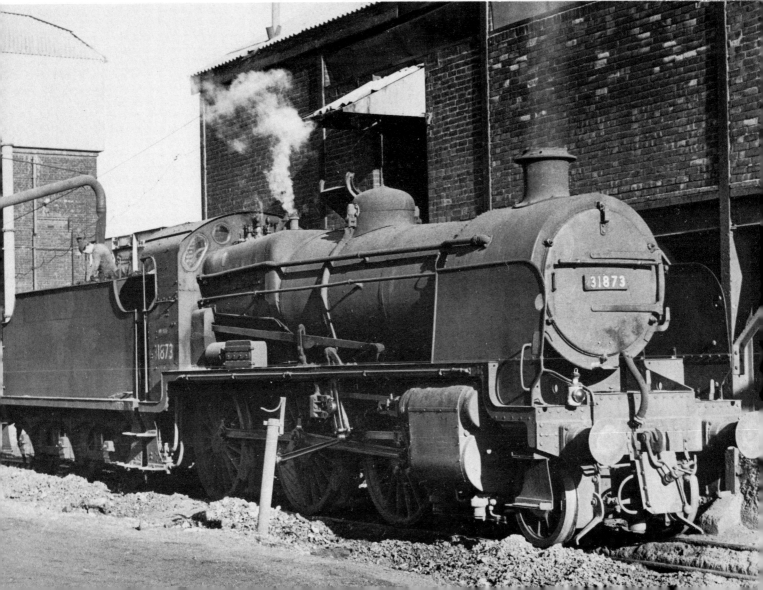

PORTRAIT OF 73040

Plate 11 One of the handsome Standard Class 5s is featured in this and the next two photographs. The class had 6 ft 2 in driving wheels and a slightly higher tractive effort than the LMS 'Black Fives'. From 1951, 172 locomotives of the type were built. In smart lined black livery, with yellow tender axle boxes, No. 73040 passes Patricroft station signalbox with a long westbound haul of freight.

Plate 12 On 18th April 1968, No. 73040 has little trouble finding enough steam for this long freight at Eccles. Passing Eccles West signalbox, the train is on the slow roads of the four track Manchester to Liverpool main line.

Plate 13 A panoramic view of Patricroft, with the driver and fireman leaning out from the cab of No. 73040 as it gets to grips with a westbound freight out of the marshalling yards. Within four months not a wisp of steam would be left at Patricroft.

FRATTON

Plate 16 At the semi-derelict depot are two of the splendid unmodified 'Battle of Britain' Class Bulleid Pacifics. The engines, No. 34064 *Fighter Command* and, nearest the camera, No. 34086 *219 Squadron*, will be used for the two portions of the Brighton to Plymouth through train. No. 34064 was unique in being fitted with a Giesel Ejector.

Plate 17 On 28th March 1965, one of the old LSWR M7 Class 0-4-4Ts, No. 30133, remained at Fratton, out of service with sacking over the chimney. The class had seen service on branch trains, e.c.s. workings and suburban services, in their sixty-seven year history.

Plate 14 Fratton was originally designated the code 70F, but when these photographs were taken, in March 1965, the shed was largely closed, with a role resembling little more than a stabling point. At the nearby station, a typical train from the Western Region, via Salisbury, headed by a Standard Class 4 2-6-0, leaves for Portsmouth and Southsea.

Plate 15 A study in light and shade inside the old roundhouse at Fratton. The focal point is a 'dead' Standard Class 5 No. 73169, fitted with a BRIB 4,725 gallon water tank and 7 ton capacity coal tender.

Plate 18 During 1966, the North East area around Sunderland and the River Wear was a stronghold of steam, with ancient 1906-built Worsdell-designed North Eastern Railway 0-6-0s still pounding the tracks with coal trains. In those now far off days, the author travelled from the Sussex Coast to County Durham on a single cylindered 'James' motor cycle, No. SPX 862. Nearing Ryhope Grange Junction with up coal empties is Class J27, No. 65835.

Plate 19 Most of the Class J27s were allocated to Sunderland and Tyne Dock during the mid 1960s. With only a three link chain by way of coupling, and not a brake pipe in sight, No. 65833 heads towards Seaham Colliery to pick up a load of coal. The North Sea can just be detected in the right background.

Plate 20 Running down to Ryhope Grange Junction with coal from Silksworth Colliery, the veteran 0-6-0 passes a Class K1 2-6-0, being held at signals on the line from Hartlepool. She is No. 65817, one of a hundred and fifteen J27s which were developed from the J26 Class.

CLASS J27s

Plate 21 Although photographed on 11th May 1966, this view represents a scene from a past age, with a 60 year old locomotive being bled to deliver its last ounce of effort for BR, before being consigned to the scrap heap. The driver, wearing a flat hat and with a self rolled cigarette, gets the signalman's 'right away' for a load of coal from the colliery at Ryhope, and makes for the nearby staithes.

Plate 22 With changes in the valve gear, and removal of the streamlined casing, the modified Bulleid Pacifics had a great deal to offer, yet because of the deliberate rundown in steam power, BR never got their money's worth in terms of longevity of service. Making a considerable effort on the long climb from Winchester, on 9th February 1967, is 'West Country' No. 34108 *Wincanton* with an up express for Waterloo.

Plate 23 Sir Keith Park was one of the modified 'Battle of Britain' Class locomotives to be withdrawn over a year before the end of Southern steam. With the haunting sound of its whistle wailing, No. 34053 nears Shawford with a down express comprising BR and Bulleid stock, in the late summer of 1965.

MODIFIED PACIFICS

Plate 24 Rebuilding of the Bulleid Pacifics took place from 1957, but whereas the larger 'Merchant Navy' Class were all modified, only some of the 'WC' and 'BB' Light Pacific types were so treated. In March 1966, No. 34077 *603 Squadron* roars down towards Weybridge in miserable weather, with the 'Bournemouth Belle'.

Plate 25 'West Country' No. 34034 *Honiton* is seen here in silhouette at Redbridge, west of Southampton, with a down train. The romantic names of the 'West Country' Class were taken from West Country towns served by the Southern Railway, or from Rivers, Tors, Vales and Valleys which were part of the surrounding countryside.

AROUND EDINBURGH

Plate 26 By mid-1966, Scottish steam was well on the way o
and scheduled workings were few and far between. On 24th Ju
1966, one of Edinburgh St. Margaret's proud Class V2s, N
60955, stands in the shed, clean, but out of use. The site of t
shed is now obliterated by a Sports Centre.

Plate 28 V2 Class No. 60919 was one of the last ten locom
tives of the Class to survive. Based at Dundee rather th
Edinburgh, No. 60919 was rostered to work the 18.40 Edinbur
to Dundee relief train on four consecutive evenings during Ju
1966. The class ended scheduled work on passenger trains at t
end of the summer timetable. The locomotive was photograph
at Edinburgh Waverley.

Plate 29 Blasting out of Waverley and into Princes Stre
Gardens with the 18.40 extra to Dundee, (1Z25), on 28th Ju
1966, is No. 60919. These 93 ton Gresley-designed machir
had a nominal tractive effort which was higher than that of
'Merchant Navy', but despite driving wheels of a similar si
to the 'MNs', they were not as fast and were designated 7P rath
than the 'MNs' 8P. One example only has been preserve
No. 60800 *Green Arrow*.

Plate 27 Peacefully simmering in the sun on a quiet Sund
afternoon at St. Margaret's depot, Edinburgh, is 'Black Five' N
45162. For some reason, the old steam sheds always had mc
atmosphere than today's diesel depots, even though the latter a
considerably cleaner places.

Plate 30 The men of steam were as much a part of the BR steam scene as the locomotives themselves. 'Not to be Moved' during a rare clean-up at Eastleigh, is 'West Country' 4-6-2 No. 34019 *Bideford*. Under the grime and oil, the smart lined green livery could normally be detected, and an oily rag worked wonders on special occasions.

Plate 31 The Southern Region never had water troughs, and replenishment was from water columns, making a stop obligatory. In this rare view, the crew of a Light Pacific stop the prestigious 'Bournemouth Belle', at Basingstoke, to take on water. The Pullman Car passengers were no doubt outraged at the unscheduled stop. The train has now passed into the annals of history, and although sometimes diesel-hauled, at the end the 'Belle' died with the steam engine.

Plate 32 Oily cotton waste is used to make a start on cleaning No. 34100 *Appledore*, at Salisbury motive power depot. The first clean part of the boiler is catching the light from the roof. Note the unusual Bulleid pattern wheels.

Plate 33 One of the very last B1 Class 4-6-0s was kept in good condition at Leeds Holbeck shed during its final days. On 23rd September 1967, the driver of No. 61306 walks the running plate with lubricant. Note the oil can on the step just in front of the cylinder.

Plate 34 Attention to the lubricators at Rose Grove shed on 17th April 1968, during the last four months of BR steam. The fitter is attending to a Class 8F 2-8-0 freight locomotive. These locomotives continued to work north Lancashire lines until the end came in August 1968.

Plate 35 Rose Grove (8F) was an active shed, and one of the few centres of guaranteed action in those final years of steam run-down. Performing one of the more unattractive jobs of cleaning ash out of the smokebox, is a young member of the cleaning staff, wearing accepted 'men of steam' clothing.

Plate 36 The team of driver and fireman were inseparable in the steam locomotive world. So the textbook partnership of the older experienced driver and the young fireman on his driver apprenticeship was frequently seen, as in this study of the crew watering their 'Black Five' at Newton Heath in 1966.

Plate 37 A final twist to secure the smokebox door of Class 8F, No. 48773 at Bolton motive power depot. It was usual during the last four years of steam for the shed allocation plate to be missing, presumed stolen, and for the code to be crudely painted on the locomotive, as seen here.

Plate 38   The soft three cylinder beat of 'Merchant Navy' Class 4-6-2 No. 35007 *Aberdeen Commonwealth*, and an exhaust of pure white smoke, produces a memorable sight just south of Eastleigh in April 1965. The leading green coach is Bulleid type No. S66S, and the train is London bound.

Plate 39   No. 35030 *Elder Dempster Lines* was once withdrawn from service, but later re-instated when BR found themselves temporarily short of power. Although in really dirty condition, the old girl tries to show her paces with a respectable eleven coach load, as she passes Basingstoke shed with a train for the capital.

THE 'MERCHANT NAVY' CLASS

Plate 40 No. 35007 *Aberdeen Commonwealth* was allocated to Salisbury depot when photographed towards the end of 1964, just east of Farnborough, with a down semi-fast train. Towards the end of the steam era, several drivers were prepared to 'have a go' with these run-down locomotives, and speeds in excess of 100mph were recorded where the line maximum speed should have been 90mph.

Plate 41 A respectably clean No. 35023 *Holland-Afrika Line*, forges westward down the LSWR main line between Woking and Brookwood, during the last month of steam on the Southern Region, July 1967. The telephoto lens compresses the 98 ton bulk of the locomotive.

Plate 42   A fitter's nightmare, with steam coming from every joint of No. 35013 *Blue Funnel*, as it tries fruitlessly to gain speed with an up train at Eastleigh. Only steam locomotives, with their simple but robust structure and design, could have soldiered on in such condition, but to the eyes of those who remembered the old days, sights such as this were pathetic.

Plate 43   The 'Merchant Navy' Class were all named after well known shipping lines. On 27th August 1966, No 35029 *Ellerman Lines* looks really impressive in this study on the Northam Curve near Southampton, with an up express. This locomotive was saved from oblivion by the National Railway Museum, but only to be 'sectioned' (i.e. almost cut in half) to expose its working parts. Let us hope that this will contribute to the education of future generations.

THE Q1 CLASS

Plate 44 The 'Austerity' Class Q1 0-6-0s of the Southern Railway were built during the Second World War, and the design of the forty locomotives was essentially simple in the interests of economy. Nevertheless, Bulleid produced an extremely powerful locomotive. In the winter of 1964/5, one of the few survivors runs through the snow in Guildford Yard, its number, 33020, curtailed to the original C20.

Plate 45 It was not always an easy matter to get Q1 haulage on passenger trains. During the last week of steam operation on the Reading to Redhill and Tonbridge line, No. 33006 passes underneath the LSWR main line at Farnborough with a Redhill train, on 28th December 1964. One of the class has been preserved, and is running on the Bluebell Railway in Sussex.

AROUND OXFORD

Plate 46 Just before the end of steam on the Western Region in December 1965, the GWR's 'Black Five', Collett-designed 'Hall' Class 4-6-0 No. 5971 *Merevale Hall*, fights for adhesion on the frost covered tracks at Oxford, with an up parcels train. The fine old semaphore signals have long been dispensed with.

Plate 47 One of the popular Class 61XX 2-6-2 Prairie Tanks, No. 6135 clanks past Culham on its way to Oxford. Together with Southall and Old Oak Common, Oxford depot was a last outpost of GWR steam when operations ceased on 31st December 1965.

Plate 48 A Midland interloper rumbling up from Banbury, in the shape of LMS Class 5MT No. 44869, threads the trackwork of Oxford, before the station was rebuilt. She hauls a freight for Reading. Note the profusion of manual signals, and the water towers beside the track.

Plate 49 One of the last 'Grange' Class 4-6-0s No. 6849 *Walton Grange*, seen here nameless, passing Oxford station, light engine, on its way to the depot. It was photographed on 22nd November 1965, and within five weeks every trace of steam had gone, save for derelict lines of silent engines.

WAR DEPARTMENT
2-8-0s

Plate 50 The 'WD' description of the Class stood for War Department, as the locomotives were introduced in 1943 to a Riddles design, and purchased in 1948 by the new British Railways Board. The locomotives were of 2-8-0 and 2-10-0 types, but the former were superior locomotives in every way. The class were true workhorses, and for 25 years they handled much of BR's freight with little limelight or publicity. No. 90135 was photographed at Wakefield Kirkgate in May 1966.

Plate 51 A grubby 'WD' Class 2-8-0 steams towards Wakefield at Oakenshaw Junction, with westbound coal for Healey Mills Yard. This area now sees a fraction of the freight traffic which traversed the freight line complexes in the mid 1960s.

Plate 53 Passing along the restriction infested line through Billingham-on-Tees with a train for the Stockton-on-Tees area in May 1966, is No. 90011. The dimensions of the 'WDs' were very similar to the 'LM' Class 8F 2-8-0s, and both had 4ft 8½in driving wheels, 225lb boiler pressure and Walschaerts valve gear.

Plate 54 Towards the end of Eastern Region steam, Wakefield was a mecca for 'WD' enthusiasts. Here No. 90615, fitted with small snowplough attachment, passes a fine gantry of ten signals at Calder Bridge Junction with a mixed load of four wheeled coal wagons, on 12 May 1966.

Plate 52 Doubtful quality coal for No. 90370 as it darkens the skies of Wakefield whilst crossing the River Calder. Well over 700 of these engines were built, but only a single 2-10-0 from the Army has survived for posterity.

'JUBILEE' CLASS

Plate 55 One of Stanier's smart three cylinder express engines wheezes out its last days on humble freight duty between Wakefield and Normanton. One of the last nine 'Jubilee' Class engines to survive was No. 45694 *Bellerophon*. The yellow stripe on the cab side indicates that the Class was not permitted to run beneath the LMR 25 kV overhead catenary.

Plate 56 Just days before the locomotive was withdrawn from service, 'Jubilee' Class No. 45608 *Gibraltar* runs tender first, with a handful of wagons, over a viaduct on a freight siding adjacent to the abandoned Leeds Central station. Note the customary steam leaks around the cylinders.

Plate 57 Newton Heath depot (9D), was one of the most active steam centres in the Manchester area in the final year or two of BR steam. In this view, taken from within the depot, a fitter's mate earns a rest whilst clearing ash.

A LOOK AT NEWTON HEATH

Plate 58 A typical view of the old shed, with two Class 8Fs standing either side of one of the substantial water columns, and an established member of the workforce with characteristic uniform, passing No. 48368.

Plate 59 The complex looking coaling system at Newton Heath, with two corrugated tin towers being dwarfed by the vast concrete structure behind. Amongst piles of coal dust and ash, 'Black Five' No. 44861 is piled high with fuel during a depot visit in June 1967.

Plate 60 A brace of 'Black Fives' in the shape of No. 45246 of Newton Heath, and No. 45347 of Lostock Hall, Preston, were both in steam when photographed on 8th June 1967.

Plate 61 A housing estate now covers
...acres of sidings which could be found
...th of Newton Heath depot. With
...ders working overtime, No. 44697
...ts for a grip under her six driving
...eels, in an attempt to shift a line of
...demned coaches from the tightly
...ved sidings.

Plate 62 With dusk setting in, a 'Black
...e' headed parcels train makes for
...chdale, on the lines of the old
...ncashire and Yorkshire Railway.

Plate 65 By August 1968, all was quiet at Newton Heath. The only serviceable locomotives had been steamed for the last time, and most of the remaining machines had a number of parts missing, mainly due to cannibalisation for spares as the stores ran dry.

Plate 63 The Newton Heath shed structure was a mixture of brick, wood and asbestos, with an iron girder or two. Centre of attraction is No. 44818, but No. 44864 on the left seems to be the only locomotive with anything resembling a shine about it.

Plate 64 The most common locomotive types in the Manchester area, towards the end of steam, were the Class 5MT 4-6-0s and Class 8F 2-8-0s. There are at least nine of Stanier's products in this general view of the shed, taken in September 1967, whilst on the right is the modern diesel depot, with a d.m.u. just visible.

Plate 66 Although in Plate 63 No. 44818 had been in steam, by 1st August 1968 it was dead, in common with its sister engine, No. 45203. Chalked on the tender of No. 44818 was the inscription 'reserved for the Keighley and Worth Valley Railway' but the locomotive was not saved. Thirteen other engines of the class were preserved, including one on the KWVR.

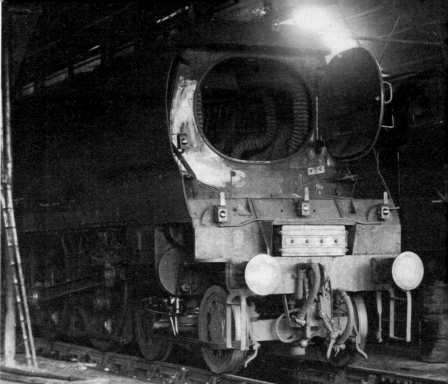

BITS OF A BULLEID

Plate 67 The motion of the third (middle) cylinder of the unmodified 'WC' and 'BB' Class Light Pacifics gave considerable trouble on some locomotives. This 1965 photograph shows No. 34079 *141 Squadron* at its home depot of Eastleigh, with all its cylinders stripped down.

Plate 68 Boiler tubes, blastpipe, and a variety of other ducts are exposed for the world to see on this unmodified 'West Country' at Eastleigh. Note also the a.w.s. equipment and electric indicator lighting on the front end.

Plate 69 A full set of 6 ft 2 in driving wheels with new tyres, waiting to be fitted to No. 34025 *Whimple*, in Eastleigh Works during the latter part of 1965.

Plate 70 One of the last modified 'West Country' Class 4-6-2s to receive a heavy overhaul at Eastleigh Works, was No. 34025 *Whimple*. At the end of steam, Eastleigh survived Ashford, Brighton and Lancing as the last Works to deal with steam engines on the Southern Region, although Lancing was primarily a carriage works.

THE LYMINGTON BRANCH

Plate 71   Through the woods near Wellworthy Ampress Works Halt, is Standard 2-6-4T No. 80138 on 23rd February 1966. Two coaches were normally more than adequate for the branch, but traffic was sufficient for BR to electrify the branch in 1967, possibly to accommodate the Isle of Wight boat traffic, rather than locals visiting Brockenhurst or Southampton.

Plate 72   Having run round its coaches at Brockenhurst, No. 80138 travels bunker first on its way to Lymington Pier, which is about 4½ miles from the junction with the main line and 5½ miles from Brockenhurst.

Plate 75 Unusual lower quadrant signals, large wooden framed crossing gates, and green enamel Lymington Pier sign, date this scene on the branch. No. 80016 simmers at the terminus whilst the crew, on the right of the photograph, have a chat on 25th October 1966.

Plate 73 In this photograph, taken in March 1967, the third rail had been placed in situ for the forthcoming electrification. Steaming through the leafless trees of the New Forest is No. 80146 with an up train.

Plate 74 Another 2-4-6T on the Lymington service, photographed on the afternoon school train at Brockenhurst. The tank is taking on water before heading west into the setting October sun.

Plate 76 On 25th October 1966, No. 80016 crosses Lymington Harbour, above the yachts lying at anchor, with a Brockenhurst to Lymington Pier train. The Pier is conveniently situated on the banks of the Solent, and there are regular sailings for Yarmouth on the Isle of Wight, which is only 4 miles across the water.

FROM ROSE GROVE TO COPY PIT

Plate 77 This four page section shows freight activity between Rose Grove and Copy Pit, on the line between Accrington and Todmorden, originally part of the old Lancashire and Yorkshire Railway. Passing Rose Grove West Junction with a string of coal empties, is Class 5MT No. 45447. The train has come from Accrington, and the branch behind the train goes to Padiham Power Station.

Plate 79 Coming off the Skipton line at Gannow Junction with an up parcels train, which includes a Western Region Siphon C vehicle, is No. 44809. Note the chimneys of the typical Lancashire mills.

Plate 80 Class 8F from Heaton Mersey, No. 48365 earns a short breather with a massive coal train before it runs into Rose Grove past some quite remarkable Lancashire and Yorkshire wooden signals, which are of the lower quadrant type. Most of the sidings in this area have now been lifted.

Plate 78 The coupling rods of No. 45435 clank past Rose Grove West signalbox with a freight for Skipton, which would be routed via the now closed through route via Colne. Note the shed and coaling tower of Rose Grove depot (10F) in the background.

Plate 83 Men at Work — says the headboard, which would seem to have a greater affinity with road transport than the BR scene. With a panorama of Rose Grove Yard behind, No. 48167 emits white plumes of smoke, as it marshalls its train of coal in April 1968.

Plate 81 The goods yard scene of yesteryear, with loose coupled and vacuum braked four wheeled wagons and no sign of the block load vehicles of the 1980s, with their roller bearings and air brakes. With a steady rhythmic beat, Class 5MT No. 45397 heads for Copy Pit, whilst a Class 8F 2-8-0 with a number which is simply too dirty to read, shunts wagons in the yard. Photographed on 7th April 1978.

Plate 82 Passing the platforms of Rose Grove with a load of coal from Yorkshire, is No. 48527. In the background, the facing wall of the terraced houses advises the community to 'insist on Duttons Ales'. The distant hill is Pendle Hill, 1,831 ft high.

Plate 84 In disgusting external condition, No. 48167 does a Class 08 shunter's work at Rose Grove. There was little point in cleaning machinery which would be scrapped within 14 weeks or so. The station behind has now been reduced in accommodation to little more than a glorified bus shelter.

Plate 85 The slog over the Pennines to Copy Pit was a severe test for man and machine, and this Class 5MT No. 45447, was travelling at little more than walking pace, even though its long train consisted of empty wagons. The author can still recall the sound of the exhaust against the hills behind.

Plate 86 In miserable weather, No. 45447 finally clears the summit at Copy Pit, and will now enjoy a descent through Portsmouth, Lancashire. Note the line of wagons, indicating how the gradient falls away under the bridge.

PATRICROFT

Plate 87 Total silence on 1st August 1968 at Patricroft, shortly after the last fire had been dropped. Standing in complete stillness are two Class 8Fs, and on the right, Standard Class 5 No. 73050. The Standard was to be the only example of its class with standard valve gear to be preserved. It is now called *City of Peterborough* and it can be seen in action on the Nene Valley Railway, near Peterborough.

Plate 88 Beneath an intricate pattern of beams and pipes forming the roof of Patricroft shed, is Class 8F No. 48374. The locomotive has had its motion partly dismantled, and within a few weeks it would be towed to the breakers' yard.

Plate 91 Only days after Patricroft closed to steam, the vandals moved in. No. 73143 is seen through the broken glass of an outbuilding in Patricroft Yard on 1st August 1968.

Plate 89 Patricroft had two major shed buildings housing locomotives, roughly in an 'L' formation. Although the 'fifteen guinea Special', commemorating the end of steam had yet to run, the end had already come for Patricroft when this photograph was taken.

Plate 90 'Britannia' Pacific No. 70004 *William Shakespeare* once headed the 'Golden Arrow' and had gleaming paintwork, but in this September 1967 shot, she was near the end of her working life. The locomotive was one of the last dozen 'Britannias' to survive. No. 70004 is simmering in front of Patricroft's coaling tower.

Plate 92 On 18th April 1968, Class 8F No. 48493 is reduced almost to a silhouette against the stormy sky, as it gently puffs away from the Patricroft area with a freight for Liverpool.

GLASGOW TO ADERDEEN

Plate 95 Keeping time with one of the 3 hour Glasgow to Aberdeen expresses, is Class A4 No. 60034 *Lord Faringdon*, the last of the Class to receive a major overhaul. With its three cylinders fighting the bank out of Dunblane, the graceful streamliner makes for Gleneagles and Perth in July 1965.

Plate 93 Leaving Forfar just 14 minutes in front of the 'Bon Accord' in July 1965, is the 06.20 Aberdeen to Perth stopping train. Blasting away from the station is No. 44703 at precisely 07.50 in the morning. The line was subsequently abandoned as a passenger route in 1967.

Plate 94 'Peppercorn' Class A2 4-6-2 No. 60532 *Blue Peter* makes steady progress out of Perth with the up 'Grampian' 3 hour Aberdeen to Glasgow express on 27th July 1966. At this time, only Nos. 60528/30/32 survived, with No. 60532 being shedded at Aberdeen Ferryhill. *Blue Peter* was subsequently preserved following an appeal by the television programme of the same name.

Plate 96 A Class 5MT with Caprotti valve gear, climbs away from Dunblane with a clear chimney, on a Glasgow to Aberdeen semi-fast train. No. 73154 of St. Rollox shed is hauling a rake of standard BR rolling stock in maroon livery. Journey times between these major Scottish cities has improved by only 5 minutes since the days of steam, although trains now travel via Dundee and make more scheduled stops en route.

AT CARNFORTH

Plate 97 Carnforth was the last depot on the BR network to which Class 9F 2-10-0s were allocated. Sharing the yard with some now extinct 'Clayton' diesels is No. 92118, one of seven Class 9Fs out of 19 steam locomotives noted on 16th April 1968.

Plate 98 Framed by the massive wooden doors of Carnforth motive power depot is No. 92167, with steam up, waiting its next turn of duty. Note the improvised number plate and shed code disc.

Plate 99 A Fairburn 2-6-4T No. 42154 at Carnforth on 7th January 1965. These powerful tank engines turned the scales at 85 tons. Two preserved examples are now located at the Lakeside Railway, Haverthwaite.

Plate 100 The last steam locomotive to be outshopped from Crewe Works was 'Britannia' Class No. 70013 *Oliver Cromwell*. The locomotive was in immaculate green livery when photographed at Carnforth on 16th April 1968, an unusual sight during the final months of BR steam. Carnforth is now the home of Steamtown, a major steam preservation centre.

AROUND YORK

Plate 101 Over the ash pit at Y
motive power depot (50A) is
43071, one of the Ivatt's Class 4
2-6-0 moguls. Some thought th
locomotives were unattractive,
they were a successful design wh
was repeated on the sim
Standard 2-6-0s produced fr
1953 onwards.

Plate 102 With so much leaki
steam, it is a wonder that N
43133 found enough pressure
move this very lengthy freight, n
to mention lifting the safety valv
and thereby 'blowing off' in t
process. It was photograph
approaching Chaloners Wh
Junction in May 1965.

Plate 103 One of the Swindon designed Standard Class 3MT 2-6-0s is dwarfed by the coaling tower at York motive power depot in 1965. Only twenty of the class were constructed. Coal can be seen falling into the tender in the gap between the locomotive and the bottom chute on the tower.

Plate 104 Propelling the York motive power depot Inspection Saloon of Gresley LNER origin is No. 77012 on 5th May 1966. By this time considerable patience was needed by the photographer hoping to photograph steam in action, as the main line was firmly in the hands of diesel locomotives.

SOUTHERN TANKS AT WORK

Plate 105 Passing a chalk cutting in th Purbeck Hills at Corfe Castle, is Standar 2-6-4T No. 80094, with the 17.0 Swanage to Wareham branch train o 15th June 1966. The train seems to b full of returning holidaymakers.

Plate 106 During the last months o steam at Waterloo, two Class 4MT 2-6-4 tanks were on duty. Nos. 80154 an 80012 wait to move either empty stoc or parcels vans between Waterloo an Clapham Yard, on 24th January 1967.

Plate 108 Although numbers in the 4XXXX series were normally associated with the London Midland Region, a number of 2-6-2T and 2-6-4T locomotives were employed on the Southern Region for many years. 'Mickey Mouse' tank No. 41312 prepares to leave Wareham with the two coach Swanage branch train.

Plate 109 An impression of speed from No. 41299 on the single line from Guildford to Horsham. Photographed shortly before closure in May 1965, the 2-6-2T locomotive is nearing Baynards in the county of Surrey, with the 10.34 departure from Guildford.

Plate 107 Entering the passing loop at Corfe Castle station is No. 80094 with an up evening train for Wareham. The line closed to passengers from 3rd January 1972, but part of the line, from Worgret Junction to Furzebrook, remains open for oil trains.

ON THE SOMERSET AND DORSET

Plate 110 The Somerset and Dorset was one of the most popular railway lines in the country. However, by the period covered in this volume, the through expresses from the Midlands and the North had long gone, leaving little more than a 67 mile branch line serving a largely rural community. Only one train a week stopped at Templecombe Lower station, and it was not the 09.53 from Bath to Bournemouth seen in this photograph. Bursting from the bridge under the L&SWR main line on 7th August 1965 is No. 73068.

Plate 111 The 16.20 from Bath Green Park to Bournemouth West slows for its stop at Shepton Mallet (Charlton Road) station in August 1965. The locomotive is Class 4MT No. 75072 of Templecombe shed. Note the viaduct in the background.

Plate 112 The 11.40 Bournemouth to Bristol semi-fast train storms across Shepton Mallet viaduct, on its non-stop run of 26½ miles from Evercreech Junction to Bath. In charge of the four vehicle train is Class 4MT No. 75072.

Plate 113 A charming study of Templecombe (Upper) with No. 41296 standing by to assist trains to and from the nearby S&D Junction, whilst sister locomotive No. 41283 leaves for Evercreech Junction with a bogie utility van and a Hawksworth coach, on 27th September 1965.

Plate 114 Hard manual labour is used at Templecombe shed as four railway staff struggle with the turntable whilst turning the 63 ton 2-6-2T No. 41307. The whole of the S&D system was abandoned from March 1966, except for short stretches of track which were adjacent to other BR lines at Highbridge, Bath and Blandford Forum.

Plate 115 There was a 22½ mile branch from Evercreech Junction to Highbridge, which enjoyed up to half a dozen trains a day in each direction. This photograph shows a typical latter day branch train, headed by No. 41283 of Templecombe shed. The train is in the centre road awaiting the next turn.

Plate 116 The S&D met the Western Region Bristol to Taunton main line at Highbridge, and the station boasted a crossover to the Burnham extension, and no less than seven platforms. There was no question of a 'one engine in steam' operation, and on the occasion of this visit, in September 1965, there were two train sets and three engines in steam. No. 41290 stands at the buffer stops at Highbridge.

Plate 117 Tank engines were used even on the long Bournemouth to Bath run, and a stop at Evercreech Junction was necessary to take on water. The crew of No. 80096 feed the side tanks for the run over the Mendip Hills to Bath.

Plate 118 The end of the S&D should have come in January 1966, but it staggered on until March. This view shows Nos. 41307 and 41283 at Glastonbury, during a photographic stop on one of the premature last day specials in January 1966. They had double headed an LCGB special from Evercreech.

Plate 121 A general view of Bath shed with Class 3MT No. 82041 ready to take the next Bristol train forward, and Standard Mogul No. 76026 taking on coal before returning to Bournemouth West. By September 1965 the depot was but a shadow of itself, no longer enjoying its strategic status of the past.

Plate 119 A view of the superb all-over roof of Bath Green Park station, which is now without rails, and used as a car park. Steaming back to the running shed for turning and fuel is No. 76026, which had just headed a train from Bournemouth. The point levers in the foreground are of interest.

Plate 120 The fireman of 2-8-0 No. 48706 takes a ride to Bath S&D engine shed. The LMS type of 2-8-0 had finally taken over the meagre freight traffic from the more famous S&D Class 7F 2-8-0s during 1964.

Plate 122 Apart from the Vale of Rheidol narrow gauge engines, the 57XX Class Pannier Tanks were the last ex-GWR locomotives to remain in service, and some survived the end of Western Region steam in December 1965. The driver of No. 3681 has a read between shunting duties in the S&D sidings at Bath.

SMOKE EFFECTS

Plate 123 On 22nd November 1965, a Stanier 2-8-0 darkens the skies at Oxford whilst moving a southbound freight out of the station. The frosty conditions contribute to the smoke effect.

Plate 124 A dramatic departure from Winchester on 29th October 1966, as 'West Country' Class No. 34008 *Padstow* takes an up train for Waterloo. The third rail is already in place for the forthcoming electrification, which caused the death of Southern steam the following July.

Plate 127 With the front end ▶
of 'West Country' Class No.
34044 *Woolacombe* appear-
ing almost as a silhouette
against the plume of white
smoke, a Portsmouth to
Basingstoke parcels train
makes steady progress up the
gradient through Micheldever
station, in February 1967.

Plate 128 With the terraced ▶
houses of Brighton forming
a backcloth, No. 34108
Wincanton seems to be steaming well, as it crosses London
Road viaduct, with the last
steam train special on the
Southern's Central Division,
on 19th March 1967. The
next stop was Eastbourne.

Plate 125 With a shattering burst of the regulator, 'WD'
Class 2-8-0 No. 90135 crosses the River Calder on its way
to pick up a train at Healey Mills on 12th May 1966.

Plate 126 No worries about smokeless zones for the crew
of J27 0-6-0 No. 65788 of Sunderland, as the old locomotive fiercely attacks the climb to Seaham, just south of
Ryhope Grange Junction, in May 1966.

AROUND LINCOLNSHIRE

Plate 129 By July 1965, there was only a modicum of steam still in service around Frodingham, and this was mainly 'WD' 2-8-0s on freight service. However, 'B1' Class 4-6-0 No. 61168 was found to work this train from Cleethorpes as far as Doncaster. It is seen entering Scunthorpe station.

Plate 130 One of the lovely old Robinson Great Central Class 04/1 locomotives to survive until 1965, was No. 63658. Prior to what was probably one of her last runs, the driver of the 54 year old locomotive prepares his mount for the road at Frodingham (Scunthorpe) shed.

Plate 131 Until the end of steam on the Southern, Southampton was a mecca for the steam enthusiast, and these photographs show something of the variety of classes which could be seen during the final year or so of steam traction. On 29th September 1966, Standard 2-6-0 No. 76007 keeps a long coal train on the move at Millbrook.

SOUTHAMPTON AREA

Plate 132 An eleven bogie P&O boat train takes to the down slow road, in readiness to enter the docks at Southampton, on 29th October 1966. The motive power was unmodified 'West Country' No. 34006 *Bude*. The fifth coach is a LNER Gresley buffet car.

Plate 133 A photograph taken from a three car 'Hampshire' d.e.m.u., catching a Standard 2-6-4T running down towards Northam past Mount Pleasant Crossing. Note how the cold winter weather enhances the smoke effect.

Plate 134 A very interesting photograph showing the ornate LSWR Tunnel Junction signalbox and associated lattice posted semaphore signals, all now demolished, the lifted direct spur from Southampton Central to Terminus, and a foreign invader on an up inter-regional train, in the shape of 'Black Five' No. 45493.

Plate 135 Heavy metal at Southampton Central as a 'Merchant Navy' Pacific applies the brakes to the 15.14 Bournemouth to Waterloo train, on 27th August 1966. The locomotive is No. 35027 *Port Line*. Water will be taken before the train continues to London.

Plate 136 The severe Northam curve has always required a check rail and a slow speed restriction. Leaning to the curve with a down inter-regional train of London Midland maroon stock, is No. 34102 *Lapford*. Northam station (behind the train) is now closed.

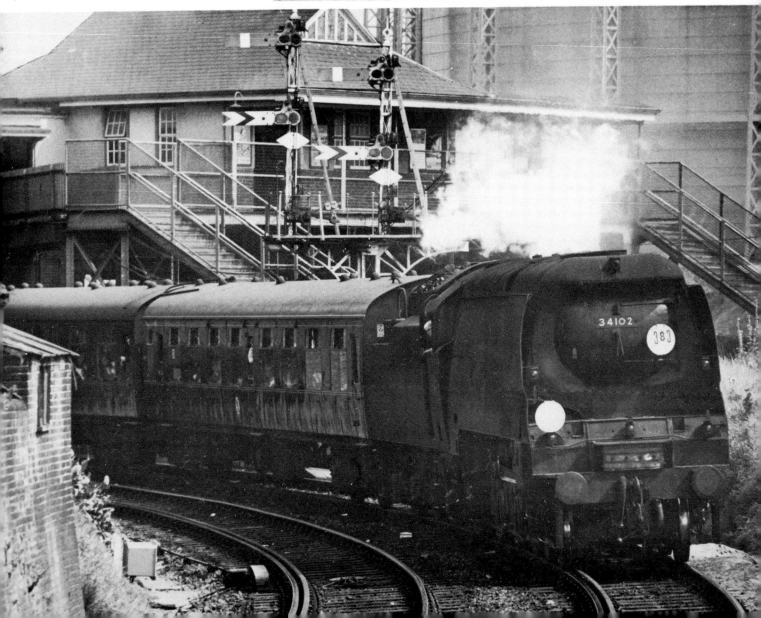

Plate 137 Framed by the Southampton west end signal gantry, and with dock crane in the background, modified Pacific, No. 34024 *Tamar Valley* sweeps around the curve, in October 1966, with an up Bournemouth to London train. At this time, the leading grey and blue coach was something of a novelty.

Plate 138 With its fairly small 5 ft 3 in driving wheels spinning like tops, No. 76066 enjoys a burst of speed as it hauls a Bournemouth to Southampton stopping train, between Redbridge and Millbrook in October 1966.

Plate 139 In her last autumn of existence, No. 75068 makes a clean and impressive start from Millbrook with a down stopping train for Bournemouth. Although this locomotive did not survive, four sister engines of the same class have been preserved.

Plate 140 One of the larger Class 5MT Standard 4-6-0s, No. 73083, leaves Southampton and heads west, past some newly installed third rail track. The third rail had not been energised at this time, but test trains were running within a few months. Photographed in the summer of 1966.

WESTERN TANKS

Plate 141 With only four weeks of Western Region steam remaining, 57XX Class 0-6-0 Pannier Tank No. 9789 passes Kennington Junction signalbox, south of Oxford, with a train of car flats for the MG Car Company Works at Abingdon.

Plate 142 One of the last Pannier Tanks to remain operative at Oxford shed was No. 9789, and this study, taken on 28th November 1965, shows the little engine on a delightful train of one brake van, heading for Abingdon to collect some MG sports cars.

Plate 143 Coming off the little used line, which once connected the Tondu to Margam route with the Cardiff to Swansea main line at Pyle, junction for Porthcawl, is one of the numerous Class 57XX 0-6-0PT locomotives, No. 9625, on 28th January 1965.

Plate 144 This volume would not be complete without a photograph of BR's only remaining steam locomotives, the Class 98s of the narrow gauge Vale of Rheidol line. This picture shows not only the original 1902 Davies & Metcalf No. 9 *Prince of Wales*, but also a 1968 scene, when trains used the old route through the present car park and the back streets of the town in a large semi-circle, before running parallel with the main ex Cambrian line to Dovey Junction.

SCOTTISH AND EASTERN 4-6-2s

Plate 147 The Class A1 Pacifics were introduced from 1945 onwards. Although in this photograph the 6 ft 8 in driving wheels look impressive, the class never quite had the legs of the streamlined Class A4s, even though cylinder size, boiler pressure and weight were similar. No. 60155 *Borderer* was photographed at York shed in January 1965.

Plate 148 Far away from its native land, Class A4 No. 60024 *Kingfisher* was rostered for an A4 Preservation Society special mainly over Southern Region lines, in March 1966. Passing Dorchester Junction, on the former GWR route from Weymouth, the immaculate green streamliner heads for Yeovil Pen Mill.

Plate 145 A gleaming Class A2 Pacific, No. 60532 *Blue Peter*, dips under a road bridge on the outskirts of Perth, with the up 'Grampian' on 27th July 1966. This locomotive was the last example of its class to survive, and was fitted with a double blast pipe and multiple valve regulator. It is now preserved at Dinting Railway Centre.

Plate 146 Dundee shed is the scene for Class A2 No. 60530 *Sayajirao*, a Peppercorn development of Thompson design, which was in turn based on the Gresley P2 Class. The locomotive and tender turned the scales at about 160 tons, and had a tractive effort higher than its Class A1/A3 and A4 cousins.

Plate 151 On 9th October 1966, Standard 4-6-0 No. 73002 scuttles across Eastleigh shed yard, having received water and coal on an adjacent road. The locomotive was built at Doncaster in 1951.

Plate 152 One of Maunsell's SE&CR mixed traffic N Class Moguls, No. 31842, was photographed outside Eastleigh shed on 9th April 1965. Whilst this engine was in steam and ready for the road, the much younger 'West Country' No. 34031 *Torrington*, visible in the background, was already on the scrap line.

EASTLEIGH (70D)

Plate 149 Eastleigh was always an important railway centre, with its origins exclusively in the London and South Western Railway. The steam shed was open until the end of Southern Region steam, in July 1967. This fine study shows No. 34026 *Yes Tor* sporting a 70E Salisbury shed plate. There is no doubt that the modified Bulleid Pacifics could have given many more years of reliable service, if the modernisation scheme had not been approved.

Plate 150 Eastleigh shed in its last days, with a miserable total of only 17 locomotives on the depot. From left to right the locomotives visible are Nos. 34087, 73115, 73117 and 34077.

SOUTHERN STANDARDS

Plate 155 A shattering departure from Basingstoke on 14th November 1965. Standard Class 5MT No. 73115 slips its wheels violently as it gets under way with a semi-fast train from Waterloo to Bournemouth West. These locomotives put up some sprightly performances on the Southern lines, and were extremely underrated.

Plate 153 An up inter-regional train for the Midlands and the North passes the delightful lower quadrant LSWR signals at Totton, Junction for Fawley. The train is 'The Pines Express', which was once routed over the Somerset and Dorset Railway, before traffic on that line was deliberately run down. Providing the motive power is No. 73155.

Plate 154 Proudly steaming, No. 73080 *Merlin* heads its seven green coaches, forming the Brighton portion of the through train from Plymouth, at Angmering-on-Sea in Sussex, in 1965. The steam locomotive diagrammed for this train ran light to and from Fratton each day, a total distance of about 86 miles, because it was the nearest steam shed to Brighton to retain servicing facilities for steam engines.

Plate 156 This was the last service train hauled by a steam locomotive on the Southern Region, to be photographed by the author. In those wretched final days, Standard Class 4MT 2-6-0 leaves Lyndhurst Road, in the New Forest, with an afternoon Bournemouth West to Southampton stopping train. The photograph was taken on 4th July 1967, two days after the official BR 'Farewell to Steam' was run, and some four days before the last day of steam on the Region.

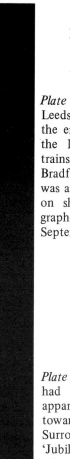

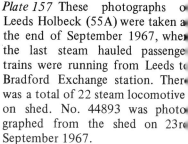

Plate 157 These photographs o Leeds Holbeck (55A) were taken a the end of September 1967, whe the last steam hauled passenge trains were running from Leeds t Bradford Exchange station. Ther was a total of 22 steam locomotive on shed. No. 44893 was photo graphed from the shed on 23r September 1967.

Plate 159 Sheds such as Holbec had a tremendous atmosphere apparent in this shot lookin towards the central turntable Surrounded by 'Black Fives' i 'Jubilee' Class 4-6-0 No. 4556 *Alberta*. At one time, it wa thought that *Alberta* would be pre served, and enthusiasts welcome its regular appearances on the Settl and Carlisle line during this period However, this was not to be, and like so many other fine engines, i was eventually cut up.

Plate 160 No. 45562 *Alberta*, on of the last half dozen 'Jubilees keeps company with the las serviceable Class B1, No. 61306 around the Holbeck turntable. Th B1 worked the Bradford t Heysham parcels later in the day.

Plate 158 A London Midlan Region line-up at, what was then, North Eastern Region shed. Flank ing Class 8F No. 48283 are tw Class 5MTs, No. 44943 of Holbec and No. 44694 of Bradford (Lo Moor).

'WEST COUNTRY' AND 'BATTLE OF BRITAIN' CLASS (UNMODIFIED)

Plate 161 Smoke trails from 'Battle of Britain' Class No. 34064 *Fighter Command* at Farnborough on 29th December 1964, heading a local from Basingstoke to Waterloo.

Plate 162 Unmodified 'BB' No. 34086 *219 Squadron* reverses onto the through train from Brighton to Plymouth, at the modernised Chichester station, in March 1965. At this time, one of the Bulleid Class CC electric locomotives hauled the train from Brighton, but because of the non-electrified lines beyond Havant and the Co-Co's return working on a freight, a Fratton based steam locomotive continued to Salisbury.

Plate 164 A number of unre built Light Pacifics lasted until the end of Southern steam. On what turned out to be only the first of several 'last steam train to Exeter' specials, No. 34015 *Exmouth* was especially cleaned in January 1966, and is seen here at Salisbury.

Plate 165 With its lined green livery gleaming, No. 34015 *Exmouth* arrives with a down freight at Southampton Central during partial rebuilding. The rebuilding included the demolition of the famous clock tower on the main up platform. The unused third rails reveal that the photograph was taken in the summer of 1966.

Plate 163 A main line express engine on secondary duties. No. 34102 *Lapford* approaches the city of Winchester with a long down fitted freight, comprising old generation four-wheeled wagons. A permanent way look out man scarcely turns his head at the spectacle.

AROUND SOUTHERN SHEDS

Plate 166 A photograph of Nine Elms shed (70A) on 2nd January 1965, finds one of the small Standard 2-6-2T locomotives at rest, with steam coming from at least seven different points. These engines were used on empty stock trains between Clapham and Waterloo, and on light parcels work.

Plate 169 Shoppers and commuters now park their cars on this spot. The shed at Guildford was always interesting, for whilst there were normally only a few engines on shed, the variety was tremendous. In this June 1966 view, only four locomotives can be seen, including one N Class at the back of the turntable, USA Class tank and, on the right, No. 73089 *Maid of Astolat*.

Plate 170 Three Adams LSWR tank engines, of a design dating back to 1889, are found in Ryde St. John's shed in this 196 photograph. At this time, both the Ryde to Ventnor and Ryde to Cowes lines were open. The locomotives are No. W2 *Whitwell*, No. W28 *Ashey* and No. W29 *Alverstone*.

Plate 167 The space taken up by Bournemouth shed (70F) has now been converted to a car park, but on 15th June 1966, Bulleid Pacifics ruled the roost. 'Merchant Navy' No. 35023 *Holland-Afrika Line* stands beside 'West Country' No. 34023 *Blackmore Vale*, which is now restored to running order on the Bluebell Railway.

Plate 168 Another shot of Bournemouth shed, with Standard tank. No. 80011 as the centrepiece. On the right is one of the new fangled Class 73 electro-diesels. The date is 4th June 1967.

EX LNER
CLASS B1 4-6-0s

Plate 173 Towards the end of steam in the West Riding of Yorkshire, special care was extended to No. 61306. Out of over 400 Class B1s built, only two have been preserved. No. 61306 is one of them, and it was subsequently painted green, and named *Mayflower*. This study was taken in Leeds Holbeck shed.

Plate 171 One of the last workings of a Class B1 4-6-0, at a time when only three of the class remained in capital stock, was on 23rd September 1967, when No. 61306 left Bradford Forster Square, in miserable conditions, with the 15.14 parcels to Heysham.

Plate 172 Leaving the neat platforms of Stirling with a stopping train for Edinburgh on 6th July 1965, is No. 61307 of Dalry Road depot. Scotland enjoyed a great deal of Class B1 activity, although there were many complaints about the steaming ability of the Class, compared with the LMS 4-6-0s.

Plate 174 An unidentified Class B1 makes a pleasant profile on the Tay Bridge, as it heads south with coal empties on 25th January 1965. The Class B1s were a Thompson mixed traffic design, dating back to the Second World War.

Plate 177 One of the powerful Class 61XX Prairie tank engines, delivered from 1931 for use on the suburban services out of Paddington, stands outside Southall shed. They weighed over 78 tons and had a 225 lb boiler pressure, combined with two large 18 in by 30 in cylinders and 5 ft 8 in driving wheels to provide rapid acceleration after frequent stops at suburban stations.

Plate 175 Even in this apparently dilapidated condition, 'Castle' Class 4-6-0 No. 5042 Winchester Castle still worked the 6.15 Paddington to Bicester and Banbury on occasions. However, by this time, the glory had gone, the paint had faded, and the copper was tarnished. The engine was on Southall shed on 19th June 1965.

Plate 176 'Hall' Class 4-6-0 No. 5971 Merevale Hall outran most of her 300 odd sister engines, and ended her days between Southall and Oxford. Although subsequently removed, the brass cabside number plate, carried by all GWR locomotives, was still in situ here, about 6 months before the end of Western Region steam.

Plate 178 It is by chance that two of the three locomotives in this line up were preserved. On the left is 'Modified Hall' No. 6998 Burton Agnes Hall, then 'Hall' No. 5971 Merevale Hall, whilst on the right is 2-6-2T No. 6106. Nos. 6998 and 6106 can now be found at the Great Western Society's Didcot Centre.

AROUND THE GWR DEPOTS

Plate 179 A locomotive in steam behind this 43XX Class 2-6-0 gives the impression that No. 7318 is in steam, whereas, in January 1965, the engine was very much on the scrap line at Gloucester shed. Some of these GWR Moguls dated back to 1911, and all were of Churchward design.

Plate 180 Another January 1965 shot, this time of a heavy freight 2-8-0 of the 28XX Class. No. 3814 is seen in front of the sizeable water tank at Newport, Ebbw Junction shed (86A). Nearly all the Class had been withdrawn by the period covered in this volume.

Plate 181 This class of Pannier tank was designed by Hawksworth for heavy shunting, but this locomotive was born into the world of British Railways and never belonged to the GWR. No. 9495 of the 94XX Class was captured on film at Old Oak Common. The 'Bluebell Line' seems to be getting some free publicity from the writing in the grease on the tank sides!

Plate 182 It would appear that 'Hall' Class No. 6926 *Holkham Hall* had just worked train number 1V25. When photographed at Old Oak Common in December 1964, the engine was allocated to 2A which was Tyseley, the GWR's main shed in the Birmingham area.

Plate 183 Visions of what used to be. 'Castle' Class No. 5042 *Winchester Castle*, in steam on Old Oak Common shed beside one of the four massive turntables, catches a last glimpse of the winter sun on 2nd January 1965. Her race was all but run.

THE SPECIALS

Plate 186 Steam on the Berks and Hants line is now becoming a very distant memory. Although her nameplates were missing, 'Modified Hall' No. 6963 *Throwley Hall* was specially cleaned for the LCGB 'Wessex Downsman' tour over the Somerset and Dorset line. The Western Region locomotive on Southern Region stock is seen at Patney and Chirton station, now closed, during a special photographic stop in April 1965.

Plate 184 A final run for one of the later Maunsell designed Class S15 locomotives. Leaving Eastleigh in light snow on 16th January 1966, is No. 30837, with the LCGB 'S15 Commemorative Railtour'. The tour had to be repeated to cope with the numbers hoping to book a seat. No. 30837 worked out of the now abandoned Feltham shed.

Plate 185 Emerging into the sunshine from the darkness of the Clayton Tunnel (1 mile 499 yards), on the main London to Brighton line, is 'West Country' Class No. 34108 *Wincanton*, with 'The Southern Rambler' tour. This was the last steam train on the line — 19th March 1967.

Plate 187 The same locomotive is seen in the classic setting of Bristol Temple Meads, before being detached in favour of a Class 4F 0-6-0 which, to the annoyance of the steam fans, had to be assisted over the bank at Fishponds by a 'Hymek' diesel hydraulic locomotive.

Plate 188 Highly polished lined black livery is discovered on Standard 2-6-4T No. 80041 waiting at Seaton Junction to take a portion of the LCGB 'East Devon' tour down the branch line to Seaton. At least 7 of these tough, mainly Brighton built tanks have been preserved, and some are still being rescued from Barry scrap yard.

Plate 189 Real lineside photography near Botley in Hampshire, as Modified 'BB' Class 4-6-2 No. 34052 *Lord Dowding* speeds by with a clear chimney, on the SCTS 'Four Counties Special' on 9th October 1966. Note the splendid lattice post and distant signal.

Plate 190 Bristol Barrow Road managed a fine external clean for Class 4F No. 44466 on the LCGB 'Wessex Downsman' tour on 4th April 1965. Internally, she was short of steam, but managed the downhill run from Mangotsfield, (seen here), to Bath Green Park.

Plate 191 Weymouth shedded 'Merchant Navy' No. 35022 *Holland-America Line* had just attained a speed in excess of 95 mph through Gillingham with the LCGB 'East Devon' tour, and had also set a new record for the Southern Region, in travelling without a water stop for 122¾ miles from Waterloo to Yeovil Junction. However, in this picture at Axminster (for Lyme Regis), more water is taken on board for the run to Exeter.

Plate 192 An unmodified 'Spam Can' was provided for the LCGB 'Vectis Farewell' tour, on 3rd October 1965, in the shape of No. 34002 *Salisbury*, seen entering Chichester station. Before proceeding to the Isle of Wight, the participants enjoyed a round trip on the Lavant branch, behind a pair of Q1 Class engines.

Plate 193 How different is this April 1968 scene, compared with the present West Coast Main Line with its overhead catenary and colour lights. On home ground is Lostock Hall's No. 48476 passing beneath the signal gantries with a medium length freight for the North.

Plate 194 A grim reminder of Preston's industrial past, as one of Stanier's products shows its smoke-box between the factory walls, and heads north with a freight for Carlisle.

PRESTON SCENES

Plate 195 Travelling through the pouring rain at some considerable speed, is Class 5MT No. 44963 with a Heysham to Warrington goods. The author was sheltering in Barton and Broughton signalbox, between Lancaster and Preston, on 16th April 1968. Needless to say, the box has since been demolished.

Plate 196 The driver of No. 44894, together with a footplate Inspector, keep an eye on the photographer's activities at the south end of Preston station. Only a 16 week period was to pass before steam on BR finished for ever.

Plate 197 Although most photo graphers pray for sunshir gloomy and rainy weather som how added to the gener depression of sheds during t declining years of steam. On very murky day, Class 8F N 48400 takes water at Losto Hall shed, near Preston.

Plate 198 Inside the shed, N 45345 manages to keep dry, b is no doubt wondering wheth it will ever be steamed agai The date is 16th April 1968.

Plate 199 The Isle of Wig lines on the Southern Regio were quite delightful to all wl knew them, and it seemed th the processes of time had bee slowed down beyond the wate of the Solent. Victorian engin and Edwardian carriages were everyday use until the last da of 1966. In this view, Class C 0-4-4T No. W16 *Ventnor* stand appropriately, at Ventnor, wi St. Boniface Down behind.

Plate 200 Havenstreet is a station which was closed when the Newport and Cowes section ceased operations on 21st February 1966. However, it was re-opened when the Wight Locomotive Society based their preserved Class O2 there a few years later. It is now the site of a preservation centre. With the weeds growing high, No. W27 *Merstone* pauses at the platform on its way to Cowes on 26th March 1965.

Plate 201 One of the Island's Class O2s hardly shows its great age while vigorously attacking the bank out of Ryde St. John's with a train for Shanklin. The train is working wrong line due to engineering works connected with the forthcoming electrification.

Plate 202 A charming study of the old order at Ryde Pier. A Class O2 hurries towards Ryde Esplanade with the 10.18 train for Cowes, whilst on the right, another Class O2 prepares to back onto the 10.25 service for Ventnor. Converted pre-war underground stock now runs over these lines, but to Shanklin only. The track layout has been substantially altered since this photograph was taken in August 1965.

Plate 203 The last four miles of the Ryde to Ventnor line, from Shanklin to Ventnor, closed during April 1966 as BR had no intention of electrifying beyond Shanklin, and rumours were circulated that the long tunnel under St. Boniface Down required heavy works. Leaving Wroxall with a down train is No. W17 *Seaview*. Wroxall, the only intermediate station between Shanklin and Ventnor, is of interest because it had a public bar on the platform.

Plate 204 Very rarely photographed was the daily Newport to Cowes parcels train. Waiting in the bay platform at Newport is Class O2 No. W21 *Sandown*, in mid 1965. The train comprises two old SR utility vans. Newport was once a busy junction with lines to Sandown and Freshwater, as well as Cowes.

Plate 205 A slightly unusual view of a Class O2 at Newport, taken from the overbridge. Note the tools of the trade on the side tanks, the poker, long shovel and bucket. The engines had Westinghouse brakes fitted for the Isle of Wight in 1923, and their bunkers were enlarged from 1932. The all-up weight was 48½ tons.

Plate 206 A pleasant August day in 1965 finds No. W27 *Merstone* ejecting steam on the approach to Ryde St. John's station. It is interesting to see what appears to be an ex works coach behind the engine, even though steam and the ancient LB&SCR and SE&CR coaches were to be withdrawn within 16 months.

Plate 207 All of the Island's locomotives were facing the same way in the mid 1960s, with the chimneys in the down direction. Therefore this shot must show an up train, because the bunker is leading. In fact, No. W28 *Ashey* was leaving Havenstreet for Ryde Pier Head. Note the small, neat, red-backed brass nameplate.

Plate 208 The locomotive that pulled BR's final steam train out of Liverpool Lime Street, on 11th August 1968, was no less than No. 45110. Known as the '15 Guinea Special', the train ran from Liverpool to Manchester/Manchester to Carlisle/Carlisle to Liverpool, a 314 mile, 10¾ hour spectacular behind four different locomotives. On 17th April 1968, the engine is seen in normal everyday service at Bolton Motive Power Depot. Later named *R A F Biggin Hill*, the locomotive can still be seen on the Severn Valley Railway.

Plate 209 The massive concrete coaling tower at Bolton makes Class 5MT No. 44929 look almost insignificant. Also worthy of a mention is the upturned brazier in front of the water tower. These were used to stop the water from freezing during cold spells in the winter.

Plate 210 On shed the same day as No. 45110, was another preserved locomotive now stabled at Bridgnorth, the 8F Preservation Society's No. 48773. The yellow diagonal stripe across the cab signified that the locomotive was not permitted to work under the overhead wires, which were then in situ south of Crewe, and between Crewe and Manchester. Class 8Fs were not normally barred.

COUNTY DURHAM EAST

Plate 211 One of the Raven designed North Eastern Railway Class Q6 0-8-0s ambles down from Cemetery North Junction towards Hartlepool. Some of these outside cylindered engines dated back to 1913, and even in the early 1960s, all 120 locomotives were still running. Pictured on 11th May 1966, No. 63406 was on the withdrawn list for the period ended 13th August 1966.

Plate 213 Although the K1 Class 2-6-0s looked fairly slight, they weighed more than the Class Q6 0-8-0s. Darlington's No. 62008 takes to the Sunderland line at Ryhope Grange Junction, with a northbound coal train.

Plate 214 Only eight weeks before Class 9F No. 92062 was given the chop, it was photographed wheezing its way past Ryhope with a Tyne Dock train. Ironically, the Class 25 diesel in the foreground, No. D5180 (later No. 25030), has also been withdrawn from service.

Plate 215 A general view of Ryhope Grange Junction, south of Sunderland, with a K1 Class 2-6-0 passing and a Class Q6 waiting in the distance. The lines to the right go to the South Dock and the staithes, and to the left to Sunderland and Newcastle.

Plate 212 Doubtful coal, or very hard work, caused the output from Class 9F No. 92063's chimney to darken the skies over Ryhope Grange Junction. With shunter's pole on the buffer beam, the large 2-10-0 heads a loaded coal train up from Sunderland South Dock. The Tyne Dock Class 9Fs were normally found on Consett iron ore trains, and they were fitted with air pumps to open the hopper doors. This picture was taken in May 1966, and the Consett steam workings finished on 19th November 1966.

Plate 216 A total of 172 Standard Class 5MTs were constructed, and thirty of them were fitted with Caprotti valve gear. These 4-6-0s were sturdy machines, and worked every type of train in their seventeen year history. No. 73158 is about to pass Wakefield Kirkgate with a loose coupled freight for Healey Mills, in May 1966.

Plate 217 With unusual looking cylinders and a rotating shaft fitted with universal joints, the external appearance of one of the Caprotti examples shows its obvious differences, not to mention the mechanical differences and mode of operation. No. 73142 sits on Patricroft shed, which closed on 1st July 1968.

STANDARD CLASS 5s

Plate 218 The camera is deliberately zoomed towards the driving wheels of No. 73168, as a train speed of about 50mph combined with a panned camera, and a shutter speed set at a 'middle range' 1/250th sec. produces a most unusual pattern in the wheel spokes. This action picture was taken at Culham, as the Standard headed towards Oxford, in November 1965.

Plate 219 The Bournemouth to Waterloo expresses were shared with the Bulleid Pacifics, and No. 71355 climbs away from the tunnel at Southampton towards Northam with an up train in the summer of 1966. A down train disappears into the smoky cutting.

SALISBURY

Plate 220 The entrance to the steam shed at Salisbury, where a thousand railwaymen have walked. This worm's eye view up the stairs from Cherry Orchard Lane, reveals a line of Standard locomotives and a number of pre-motor car staff bicycles. The whole place was flattened by bulldozers when steam finished in 1967.

Plate 222 On 26th July 1967, there were no less than 58 dead steam locomotives on Salisbury depot. It was a dumping ground until the rusting hulks of the BR steam fleet could be removed to South Wales for scrapping. There were five USA Class tank engines in the scrap lines. By chance, these two, No. 30064 in green livery and No. 30072 in black, were both preserved, and can still be seen in action at the Bluebell Railway and on the Keighley and Worth Valley Railway. The locomotives came to England from the USA during the war, and they were of a US Army Transportation Corps design. They found employment in the docks at Southampton.

Plate 223 Two of Bulleid's giants. Standing side by side like two huge sentinels, are 'West Country' Class Pacifics Nos. 34104 *Bere Alston* and No. 34100 *Appledore,* on 6th June 1967, just four weeks before the end of operations. The ten-track shed was built in 1902, and therefore lasted 65 years.

Plate 221 An example of how not to keep a steam locomotive's motion. Thick grease and grime, with a covering of road dirt, forms a sticky mass on crucial moving parts of this Standard 2-6-4T at Salisbury.

GLASGOW WEST AND SOUTH

Plate 224 Class 4MT 2-6-4T No. 80086 of Glasgow's Polmadie shed (66A), shunts the maroon stock of a London bound express at Glasgow Central station on 10th July 1965.

Plate 225 Arriving at Port Glasgow with a real assortment of stock, is a Glasgow Central to Gourock train headed by No. 80130. At this time, July 1965, services to Gourock, on the Firth of Clyde, and Wemyss Bay, were in the hands of Standard and LMS 2-6-4Ts, Standard 2-6-0s and 4-6-0s, 'Black Fives' and even d.m.u's. The whole of the network was later converted to 25kV overhead electricity on 'Blue Train' lines.

Plate 226 Straining to the limit to shift a long train of coal empties from Ayr Harbour to the main line at Newton-on-Ayr, is Stanier Class 5MT No. 45161. The skies are blackened by the smoke, sand is being applied, and steam shrouds the entire cab. No. 45161 was allocated to Ayr shed.

Plate 227 Eighty-five tons of rusting Fairburn designed 2-6-4T locomotive has steam to spare, as it slows for its Port Glasgow stop with a train from Wemyss Bay. Just below the driver, water can be seen pouring from a rust hole in the side tank. In charge of the mixed rolling stock is No. 42259 on 10th July 1965.

WILLESDEN AND MARYLEBONE

Plate 228 Just before the shed at Willesden lost its allocation of 'Jinties' to Crewe, Nos. 47432 and 47435 were both in steam on 2nd January 1965. Over 400 of these small 0-6-0Ts were built from 1924 onwards, but they gradually had to give way to the efficient Class 08 350hp diesel shunters.

Plate 230 The 'Britannia' ▶ Class Pacifics were successful, and completely outshone their smaller 'Clan' Class sister engines. With a shine on her paintwork, No. 70021 *Morning Star* is ready for the road at Willesden shed, only a few hundred yards from Old Oak Common. Trainspotters used an adjoining canal to gain access to both sheds.

Plate 231 In its last years, the ▶ old Great Central route to London saw most classes of locomotive performing between Nottingham and Marylebone. However, in the period under review, 'Black Fives' and 'Britannias' had the monopoly. Arriving at Marylebone, in torrential rain, is Class 5MT No. 45454 of Colwick shed, although 2D signifies Banbury. The GC route was the last main line into London, and the first to be closed. The picture was taken shortly before closure, north of Aylesbury, in September 1966.

Plate 229 Great Western on the Great Central. Having worked from the Banbury direction with a train for Marylebone Goods Depot, 'Grange' Class 4-6-0 No. 6829 *Burmington Grange* revolves on the turntable, just outside the GC terminus. The author subsequently enjoyed a short footplate ride on this locomotive.

Plate 234 The steam pipe of N Class 2-6-0 No. 31866 is connected to the turntable mechanism at Redhill shed for pressure whilst the fireman controls the brake and tries to line up rail with rail. At the time of writing, only a solitary N Class survives on the Mid Hants Railway at Alresford, that one being No. 31874.

Plate 235 Redhill had the code 75B, but by the time the 1966 lists were produced, the shed no longer appeared in the operational columns. Double chimney Class 4MT No. 75066 is framed by a shattered window during a depot visit in May 1965.

Plates 232 and *233* Redhill was the last steam shed in operation on the Central Division of the Southern Region, but once the Reading to Tonbridge line was dieselised, it rapidly lost its importance. When these photographs were taken, on 24th May 1965, there was very little movement and the numbers of thirteen engines were recorded. The views on this page show Standard 2-6-4Ts, out of action and surplus to requirements.

LONDON MIDLAND REGION MISCELLANY

Plate 236 The staccato beat of Bolton's Class 8F No. 48652 echoes from nearby buildings, as the locomotive makes steady progress on the climb from Manchester Victoria to Miles Platting with an eastbound freight on 8th June 1967.

Plate 237 Having a go with some coke wagons at Stoke-on-Trent on 6th July 1965, is one of the little 'Jinty' tanks. Stoke was a busy steam centre at this time, especially on the line to Crewe. A total of seven 'Jinties' have been saved from the scrap heap by preservationists.

Plate 239 The station pilot and resident banker on the ▶ night of 17th April 1968 at Manchester Victoria, was Class 5MT No. 44735. Note the light from the fire reflected in the background, as rain trickles down the tender and the locomotive's boiler.

Plate 240 A mixed freight emerges from the gloom under ▶ Bolton Trinity Street station behind No. 45104 of Bolton shed. The whole of the ground area was covered with point levers and signal wires, which were controlled by the signal-box in the left foreground.

Plate 238 One of the remarkable Johnson designed Midland Railway Class 1F tanks, which dated back to 1878, stands in front of a 'WD' Class at Staveley shed. No. 41708, without full cab, worked on the lines serving Staveley Iron Works for years, and is seen on shed in July 1965, shortly before withdrawal.

LLANDUDNO

Plate 241 An interesting view of a 'Black Five' at Llandudno Junction shed in 1965, with its smokebox door open for maintenance, revealing tubes, blastpipe and chimney.

Plate 243 Towards the end of steam, Stockport had two sheds, 9B Stockport Edgeley and 9F Heaton Mersey. Due to heavy concentration of freight on the Buxton lines, Heaton Mersey was, from the mid 1960s, busier than its 'B' shed rival. Just beside Edgeley shed, No. 45046 passes with a down freight, whilst one of the then new Class 86 electric locomotives passes on its way to London Euston with the 1A47.

Plate 244 When this view was recorded on 19th April 1968, only ten locomotives were on Edgeley shed. A driver turns up for duty and passes Class 8F No. 48549, which would appear to be the only machine in steam, judging by the empty tracks on the left.

Plate 242 Llandudno Junction shed was extremely busy during the summer season, especially on Saturdays. On the left of this study is No. 45346, a Llandudno engine, preparing to work the special 1Z50. In the middle is a Leeds based 'Jubilee' Class No. 45562 *Alberta*, and on the right, another Stanier 4-6-0, No. 45285.

HEATON MERSEY

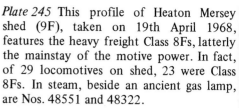

Plate 245 This profile of Heaton Mersey shed (9F), taken on 19th April 1968, features the heavy freight Class 8Fs, latterly the mainstay of the motive power. In fact, of 29 locomotives on shed, 23 were Class 8Fs. In steam, beside an ancient gas lamp, are Nos. 48551 and 48322.

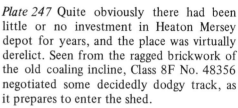

Plate 247 Quite obviously there had been little or no investment in Heaton Mersey depot for years, and the place was virtually derelict. Seen from the ragged brickwork of the old coaling incline, Class 8F No. 48356 negotiated some decidedly dodgy track, as it prepares to enter the shed.

Plate 248 Amidst acres of space around Victorian buildings, No. 48765 proves that the whole place is not dead, by creeping out towards the main line to find some work. The poor old shed looks very dilapidated and forgotten.

Plate 246 After leaving the shed, No. 48551 uses the turntable before heading out on the road to pick up a freight train. The shed was situated adjacent to the old Cheshire Lines Committee line to Liverpool, and the Midland Railway route into Manchester.

Plate 249 Gradually the end of steam came, even to those Manchester sheds which lasted almost to the last day. The four years of struggle had ended and steam had had its last gasp. Through a hole in the wall, No. 46418, one of Ivatt's Class 2MT Moguls, can be seen awaiting the final tow.

THE END OF AN ERA

Plate 250 On 1st August 1968, the last respects were paid to Newton Heath. With the weed becoming more prominent, No. 44949 has taken its final curtain, and its only value is by weight to the scrap dealer.

Plate 251 Another old soldier, minus number, coupling rods and window glass, has already given its grand finale and only the cutters' torch remains to impose the ultimate indignity. Out of some 600 machines, only two Class 8Fs were to cheat the scrap metal dealers.

Plate 252 The machinery of the past era has finally stopped, and one can only regret the policy which killed 18,000 steam locomotives within a period of a mere dozen years. Were the steam engines filthy and inefficient? Perhaps they were, but in decades to come, coal could again be king, and steam could be supreme. Whatever happens, the locomotives we knew and the classes we loved will never return.

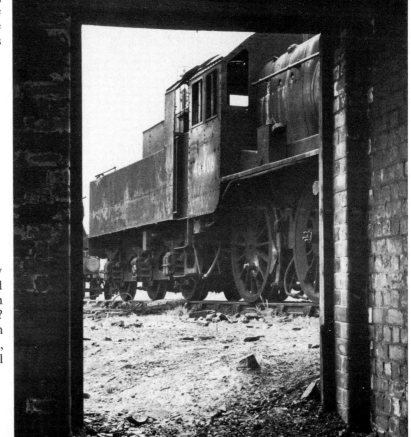

Plate 253 And so the sun went down on British steam, after a period of 140 years of service on our railways. The last four years of the period were harrowing, as the cancer of modernisation snatched shed after shed from our grasp. The pathetic sight of fine machinery, in dilapidated condition struggling to keep trains moving, was heart rending. There was no antidote for the chronic ailment, as Region by Region steam locomotives were silenced. However, despite all that, the period was unforgettable. This was not a period of gleaming machines, but a titanic struggle against all odds. There were many pleasurable moments of a personal nature. Trying to capture the period on film was a challenge that was willingly taken up. Hours upon hours were spent waiting for trains, but the emotional and psychological rewards were enormous when everything turned out just right. A way of life finished in 1968, but by the time it happened, one was almost glad, because so many ailing machines were put out of their misery. It is a strange phenomenon that we pursue the disappearing railway scene, for after steam, similar feelings were experienced on the last days of country branch lines, and, ironically, the carnage of the non-standard diesels. Whilst there is no aesthetic replacement for the steam engine, perhaps the desire to record the passing railway scene on film for the sake of posterity has filled some need. The last four years of steam have a special place, and I trust that I have been able to share those days with you, through the medium of this book.